FLORENCE NIGHTINGALE

THE FARMHOUSE BOOK CO.

Florence Nightingale

ISBN: 9798699623877

In this book, learn to care for the sick and wounded like Florence Nightingale! This book is annotated with excerpts from:
- CHILD'S HEALTH PRIMER FOR PRIMARY CLASSES by JANE ANDREWS (1885)
- AMERICAN RED CROSS TEXT-BOOK ON HOME CARE OF THE SICK by JANE A. DELANO, R. N. (1918)
- HOME ARTS FOR OLD AND YOUNG. By MRS. CAROLINE L. SMITH. (1837)
- NOTES ON NURSING: WHAT

IT IS, AND WHAT IT IS NOT by
FLORENCE NIGHTINGALE.
(1859)
• SOME FAMOUS WOMEN by
LOUISE CREIGHTON (1909)

CHAPTER ONE

Florence Nightingale

Florence Nightingale, who has done so much to improve the nursing of the sick, was born on May 12, 1820, at Florence, in Italy, and was named after her birthplace. Her parents soon went back to live in England, where her father owned a country-house, called Lea Hurst, in Derbyshire. They spent their summers in Derbyshire, and in the autumn moved to Embley Park, in Hampshire, another house belonging to Mr. Nightingale. Florence grew up loving the country and the country people who lived round her home. As a little girl she was very fond of dolls, and used to pretend that they were ill, and nurse them, and bandage their broken limbs, with the

4

greatest care and skill. She was devoted to animals and had many pets for whom she cared tenderly. Once, when she was out riding on her pony, she came upon an old shepherd whose dog had had his leg hurt by some mischievous boys. The shepherd thought that there was nothing to be done but to kill the dog to put it out of its misery. But Florence begged to be allowed to try to cure it. The leg proved not to be broken, and Florence poulticed it so cleverly that the dog was soon well again.

Photo: London Stereoscopic Co.
Florence Nightingale.

Florence was educated at home. Her
father was very particular about her studies,
and she learnt well and quickly. Even as a
child she loved to visit sick people, and as
soon as she was grown up, she spent most of
her time in the cottages and in the village
school. The old and the sick loved her visits,
and her gentle, clever ways did much to ease

6

their suffering. For the children, she invented all kinds of amusements, and delighted in playing with them. She also held a Bible class for the elder girls. So far her life had been spent much like that of many other English girls. She was pretty and charming and known to be very clever; she had travelled a good deal, and her home-life, with parents who delighted in her and one sister to whom she was devoted, was absolutely happy. But every year her interest in nursing the sick grew stronger. She had been much impressed by meeting Elizabeth Fry, and by hearing from her of the Institute of Kaiserswerth in Germany, where deaconesses were trained for nursing the sick poor. In order to find out how the sick were nursed in her own country, she visited some of the chief hospitals, and was grieved to find what ignorant, rough women the nurses were. They had no training, and did little for the comfort of the patients; the hospitals were dirty and badly kept, and the nurses were much given to drinking. Miss Nightingale also travelled in France, Germany, and Italy to visit the hospitals. There she found things on the whole much better, as the nursing was mostly done by nuns, or Sisters of Charity, religious women who had given their lives for the service of their fellow-creatures.

CHAPTER TWO

Nerves, Teeth, and Stomach

NERVES.

HOW do the muscles know when to move?

You have all seen the telegraph wires, by which messages are sent from one town to another, all over the country.

You are too young to understand how this is done, but you each have something inside of you, by which you are sending messages almost every minute while you are awake.

We will try to learn a little about its wonderful way of working.

In your head is your brain. It is the part of

9

you which thinks.

As you would be very badly off if you could not think, the brain is your most precious part, and you have a strong box made of bone to keep it in.

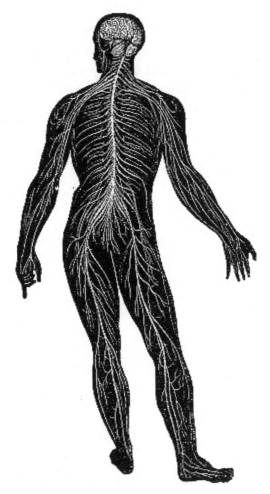

Diagram of the nervous system.

We will call the brain the central telegraph

office. Little white cords, called nerves, connect the brain with the rest of the body.

A large cord called the spinal cord, lies safely in a bony case made by the spine, and many nerves branch off from this.

If you put your finger on a hot stove, in an instant a message goes on the nerve telegraph to the brain. It tells that wise thinking part that your finger will burn, if it stays on the stove.

In another instant, the brain sends back a message to the muscles that move that finger, saying: "Contract quickly, bend the joint, and take that poor finger away so that it will not be burned."

You can hardly believe that there was time for all this sending of messages; for as soon as you felt the hot stove, you pulled your finger away. But you really could not have pulled it away, unless the brain had sent word to the muscles to do it.

Now, you know what we mean when we say, "As quick as thought." Surely nothing could be quicker.

You see that the brain has a great deal of work to do, for it has to send so many orders.

There are some muscles which are moving quietly and steadily all the time, though we take no notice of the motion.

You do not have to think about breathing, and yet the muscles work all the time, moving your chest.

If we had to think about it every time we breathed, we should have no time to think of any thing else.

There is one part of the brain that takes care of such work for us. It sends the messages about breathing, and keeps the breathing muscles and many other muscles faithfully at work. It does all this without our needing to know or think about it at all.

Do you begin to see that your body is a busy work-shop, where many kinds of work are being done all day and all night?

13

Although we lie still and sleep in the night, the breathing must go on, and so must the work of those other organs that never stop until we die.

OTHER WORK OF THE NERVES.

The little white nerve-threads lie smoothly side by side, making small white cords. Each kind of message goes on its own thread, so that the messages need never get mixed or confused.

These nerves are very delicate little messengers. They do all the feeling for the whole body, and by means of them we have many pains and many pleasures.

If there was no nerve in your tooth it could not ache. But if there were no nerves in your mouth and tongue, you could not taste your food.

If there were no nerves in your hands, you might cut them and feel no pain. But you could not feel your mother's soft, warm hand, as she laid it on yours.

14

One of your first duties is the care of yourselves.

Children may say: "My father and mother take care of me." But even while you are young, there are some ways in which no one can take care of you but yourselves. The older you grow, the more this care will belong to you, and to no one else.

Think of the work all the parts of the body do for us, and how they help us to be well and happy. Certainly the least we can do is to take care of them and keep them in good order.

CARE OF THE BRAIN AND NERVES.

As one part of the brain has to take care of all the rest of the body, and keep every organ at work, of course it can never go to sleep itself. If it did, the heart would stop pumping, the lungs would leave off breathing, all other work would stop, and the body would be dead.

But there is another part of the brain which does the thinking, and this part needs rest.

When you are asleep, you are not thinking, but you are breathing and other work of the body is going on.

If the thinking part of the brain does not have good quiet sleep, it will soon wear out. A worn-out brain is not easy to repair.

If well cared for, your brain will do the best of work for you for seventy or eighty years without complaining.

The nerves are easily tired out, and they need much rest. They get tired if we do one thing too long at a time; they are rested by a change of work.

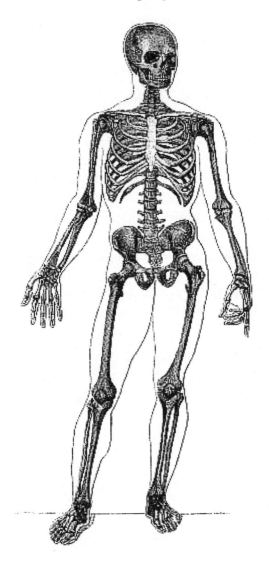

Bones of the human body.

Your teeth do not look alike, since they must do different kinds of work. The front ones cut, the back ones grind.

They are made of a kind of bone covered with a hard smooth enamel (ĕn ăm´el). If the enamel is broken, the teeth soon decay and ache, for each tooth is furnished with a nerve that very quickly feels pain.

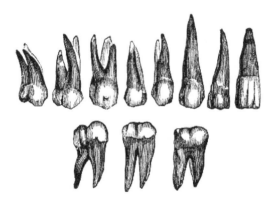

CARE OF THE TEETH.

Cracking nuts with the teeth, or even

biting thread, is apt to break the enamel; and when once broken, you will wish in vain to have it mended. The dentist can fill a hole in the tooth; but he can not cover the tooth with new enamel.

Bits of food should be carefully picked from between the teeth with a tooth-pick of quill or wood, never with a pin or other hard and sharp thing which might break the enamel.

The teeth must also be well brushed. Nothing but perfect cleanliness will keep them in good order. Always brush them before breakfast. Your breakfast will taste all the better for it. Brush them at night[63] before you go to bed, lest some food should be decaying in your mouth during the night.

Take care of these cutters and grinders, that they may not decay, and so be unable to do their work well.

THE CHEST AND ABDOMEN.

You have learned about the twenty-four little bones in the spine, and the ribs that curve around from the spine to the front, or breast-bone.

These bones, with the shoulder-blades and the collar-bones, form a bony case or box.

In it are some of the most useful organs of the body.

This box is divided across the middle by a strong muscle, so that we may say it is two stories high.

The upper room is called the chest; the lower one, the abdomen (ăb dō′měn).

In the chest, are the heart and the lungs.

In the abdomen, are the stomach, the liver, and some other organs.

THE STOMACH.

The stomach is a strong bag, as wonderful a bag as could be made, you will say, when I tell you what it can do.

The outside is made of muscles; the lining prepares a juice called gastric (găs´trĭk) juice, and keeps it always ready for use.

Now, what would you think if a man could put into a bag, beef, and apples, and potatoes, and bread and milk, and sugar, and salt, tie up the bag and lay it away on a shelf for a few hours, and then show you that the beef had disappeared, so had the apples, so had the potatoes, the bread and milk, sugar, and salt, and the bag was filled only with a thin, grayish fluid? Would you not call it a magical bag?

Now, your stomach and mine are just such magical bags.

We put in our breakfasts, dinners, and suppers; and, after a few hours, they are changed. The gastric juice has been mixed with them. The strong muscles that form the outside of the stomach have been squeezing the food, rolling it about, and mixing it together, until it has all been changed to a thin, grayish fluid.

HOW DOES ANYBODY KNOW THIS?

A soldier was once shot in the side in such a way that when the wound healed, it left an opening with a piece of loose skin over it, like a little door leading into his stomach.

A doctor who wished to learn about the stomach, hired him for a servant and used to study him every day.

He would push aside the little flap of skin and put into the stomach any kind of food that he pleased, and then watch to see what happened to it.

In this way, he learned a great deal and wrote it down, so that other people might know, too. In other ways, also, which it would take too long to tell you here, doctors have learned how these magical food-bags take care of our food.

WHAT DOES THE BODY NEED FOR FOOD?

NOW that you know how the body is fed, you must next learn what to feed it with; and what each part needs to make it grow and to keep it strong and well.

WATER.

A large part of your body is made of water. So you need, of course, to drink water, and to have it used in preparing your food.

Water comes from the clouds, and is stored up in cisterns or in springs in the ground. From these pipes are laid to lead the water to our houses.

Sometimes, men dig down until they reach a spring, and so make a well from which they can pump the water, or dip it out with a bucket.

Water that has been standing in lead pipes, may have some of the lead mixed with it. Such water would be very likely to poison you, if you drank it.

Impurities are almost sure to soak into a well if it is near a drain or a stable.

If you drink the water from such a well, you may be made very sick by it. It is better to go thirsty, until you can get good water.

A sufficient quantity of pure water to drink is just as important for us, as good food to eat.

We could not drink all the water that our bodies need. We take a large part of it in our food, in fruits and vegetables, and even in beefsteak and bread.

LIME.
Bones need lime. You remember the bone that was nothing but crumbling lime after it had been in the fire.

Where shall we get lime for our bones?

We can not eat lime; but the grass and the grains take it out of the earth. Then the cows eat the grass and turn it into milk, and in the milk we drink, we get some of the lime to feed our bones.

In the same way, the grain growing in the field takes up lime and other things that we need, but could not eat for ourselves. The

lime that thus becomes a part of the grain,
we get in our bread, oat-meal porridge, and
other foods.

SALT.

Animals need salt, as children who live in
the country know very well. They have seen
how eagerly the cows and the sheep lick up
the salt that the farmer gives them.

Even wild cattle and buffaloes seek out
places where there are salt springs, and go
in great herds to get the salt.

We, too, need some salt mixed with our
food. If we did not put it in, either when
cooking, or afterward, we should still get a
little in the food itself.

FLESH-MAKING FOODS.

Muscles are lean meat, that is flesh; so
muscles need flesh-making foods. These are
milk, and grains like wheat, corn and oats;
also, meat and eggs. Most of these foods
really come to us out of the ground. Meat
and eggs are made from the grain, grass,
and other vegetables that the cattle and hens

eat.

FAT-MAKING FOODS.

We need cushions and wrappings of fat, here and there in our bodies, to keep us warm and make us comfortable. So we must have certain kinds of food that will make fat.

Esquimaux catching walrus.

There are right places and wrong places for fat, as well as for other things in this world. When alcohol puts fat into the muscles, that is fat badly made, and in the wrong place.

The good fat made for the parts of the body which need it, comes from fat-making foods.

In cold weather, we need more fatty food than we do in summer, just as in cold countries people need such food all the time.

The Esquimaux, who live in the lands of snow and ice, catch a great many walrus and seal, and eat a great deal of fat meat. You would not be well unless you ate some fat or butter or oil.

WHAT WILL MAKE FAT?

Sugar will make fat, and so will starch, cream, rice, butter, and fat meat. As milk will make muscle and fat and bones, it is the best kind of food. Here, again, it is the earth that sends us our food. Fat meat comes from animals well fed on grain and grass; sugar, from sugar-cane, maple-trees, or beets; oil, from olive-trees; butter, from cream; and starch, from potatoes, and from corn, rice, and other grains.

Green apples and other unripe fruits are not yet ready to be eaten. The starch which we take for food has to be changed into sugar, before it can mix with the blood and help feed the body. As the sun ripens fruit, it changes its starch to sugar. You can tell this by the difference in the taste of ripe and unripe apples.

- CHILD'S HEALTH PRIMER FOR PRIMARY CLASSES by Jane Andrews (1885)

CHAPTER THREE

Declaration of War

When she was twenty-nine, Miss Nightingale decided to go herself to Kaiserswerth to study nursing. She spent only a few months there, but she was delighted with what she saw and learned. Many years afterwards she wrote: "Never have I met with a higher love, a purer devotion than there. There was no neglect. The food was poor—no coffee but bean coffee—no luxury but cleanliness." She was much loved at Kaiserswerth; and an English lady who was there eleven years afterwards was told that many of "the sick remembered much of her teaching, and some died happily, blessing her for having led them to Jesus." Miss Nightingale wrote a little book about Kaiserswerth, in which she urged that women should be encouraged to work, and should be trained properly for their work. She herself at first used the knowledge that she had gained in tending the poor who lived near her own home. After a while, she moved to London that she might be able to help in other charitable work. She was interested in a Home that had been started for sick governesses, which she heard was in a very unsatisfactory condition, and went to live there herself, shutting herself off from all society that she might care for the sick women in the Home, and arrange for its proper management. She was not at all strong, and after a time grew ill from the strain of too much work and had to go back to the country to rest.

Prayer During War.

O Lord God, who art righteous in Thy judgment, and plenteous in mercy, whose faithfulness endureth from generation to generation, who rulest even above the din of war: may all nations learn to know that Thou alone art God, that Jesus Christ is Thy

Son, and that all who truly
confess Thy name are the
people of Thy pasture and
the sheep of Thy hand. Thou
hast permitted the nations
to rise up in war against
each other and our own
beloved country to become
engulfed in its throes. O
Lord God, our Father, we
know that war is a
punishment for sin and that
we, too, have justly
merited Thy punishment
through our sins. Therefore
we humbly confess our sins,
and supplicate Thy pity and
compassion, lay not our
iniquities against us, but
graciously forgive us our
sins and shortcomings for
the sake of our Lord Jesus
Christ. To Thy fatherly
goodness and care we
commend our people, and
especially our soldiers and
sailors now in the service
of their country. They are
absent from their loved
ones, beset by dangers on
all sides. Be Thou ever
near. Keep them from all
evil. O Thou, without whose
consent not even a sparrow
falleth to the ground and

```
who hast numbered the very
hairs of our heads, take
them under the shadow of
Thy wings. Give them
courage and obedience,
fortitude and valor in the
hour of danger, and
compassion and mercy in the
flush of victory. Prosper
their arms to the
establishment of justice,
peace, and truth among all
peoples. Lead them safely
back to their homes and
their loved ones, better
citizens, better Christians
than before. And to Thy
holy name be glory, laud,
and honor, world without
end. Amen.
```

It was about this time that England and
France declared war on Russia, and the
Crimean War began. England had not been
at war for forty years, and the army was in
no way well prepared. The country rejoiced
to hear of the victory of the Alma won over
the Russians, but people learnt with
indignation of the sufferings of the soldiers
after the battle. Nothing was ready for the
care of the wounded, even food and clothing
were scarce. Letters from the Crimea told

terrible stories of the sufferings of the men. The French had fifty Sisters of Mercy to tend their sick, but the English had no female nurses. In the Times newspaper, a long letter, giving an account of the terrible state of things, was published, which ended with these words: "Are there no devoted women amongst us, able and willing to go forth to minister to the sick and suffering soldiers of the East in the hospitals at Scutari? Are none of the daughters of England, at this extreme hour of need, ready for such a work of mercy?" Many were stirred by this appeal and sent in offers of help to the War Office. Mr. Sidney Herbert, the Minister for War, was eager to send the needed help, but he felt that to send out women not trained for such work would be useless. He knew Miss Nightingale intimately, and it seemed to him that she was the one woman in England whose character and training fitted her to take the lead in this matter. He got the permission of the government to ask her to undertake the post of Superintendent of Nurses for the Crimea. Then he wrote to her to tell her the state of affairs. A large barrack hospital had been set apart for the sick and wounded soldiers at Scutari on the Bosphorus. Here the wounded were brought by ship from the Crimea. Masses of stores were being sent out, but there were no female nurses, and as women had never been employed to nurse soldiers, there were no experienced nurses ready to go, though many devoted women had offered their services. Mr. Herbert felt that there would be great difficulty in ruling the band of untrained nurses, and in making the new arrangements work smoothly with the medical and military authorities. He told Miss Nightingale that, if she would go, she should have full authority over the nurses, and the support of the government in all she might wish to do. He said that the whole success of the plan depended upon her willingness to go, and that her experience, her knowledge, her place in society gave her the power to do this work which no one else possessed. In those days it was quite a new thing to think of a lady being a nurse at all, and quite an unheard-of thing that a lady should go to nurse soldiers. Mr. Herbert thought that if this new plan succeeded, it would do an enormous amount of good both then and afterwards.

Florence Nightingale

CHAPTER FOUR

Serving Meals to the Sick

WHAT FOOD?
Common errors in diet.

I will mention one or two of the most common errors among women in charge of sick respecting sick diet. Beef tea.One is the belief that beef tea is the most nutritive of all articles. Now, just try and boil down a lb. of beef into beef tea, evaporate your beef tea, and see what is left of your beef. You will find that there is barely a teaspoonful of solid nourishment to half a pint of water in beef tea;—nevertheless there is a certain reparative quality in it, we do not know what, as there is in tea;—but it may safely be given in almost any inflammatory disease, and is as little to be depended upon with the healthy or convalescent where much nourishment is required. Again, it is an ever ready saw that an egg is equivalent to a lb. of meat, —whereas it is not at all so.Eggs. Also, it is seldom noticed with how many patients, particularly of nervous or bilious temperament, eggs disagree. All puddings made with eggs, are distasteful to them in consequence. An egg, whipped up with wine, is often the only form in which they can take this kind of nourishment.Meat without vegetables. Again, if the patient has attained to eating meat, it is supposed that to give him meat is the only thing needful for his recovery; whereas scorbutic sores have been actually known to appear among sick persons living in the midst of plenty in England, which could be traced to no other source than this, viz.: that the nurse, depending on meat alone, had allowed the patient to be without vegetables for a considerable time, these latter being so badly cooked that he always left them untouched. Arrowroot.Arrowroot is another grand dependence of the nurse. As a vehicle for wine, and as a restorative quickly prepared, it is all very well. But it is nothing but starch and water. Flour is both more nutritive, and less liable to ferment, and is preferable wherever it can be used.

Milk, butter, cream.

Again, milk and the preparations from milk, are a most important article of food for the sick. Butter is the lightest kind of animal fat, and though it wants the sugar and some of the other elements which there are in milk, yet it is most valuable both in itself and in enabling the patient to eat more bread. Flour, oats, groats, barley, and their kind, are as we have already said, preferable in all their preparations to all the preparations of arrow root, sago, tapioca, and their kind. Cream, in many long chronic diseases, is quite irreplaceable by any other article whatever. It seems to act in the same manner as beef tea, and to most it is much easier of digestion than milk. In fact, it seldom disagrees. Cheese is not usually digestible by the sick, but it is pure nourishment for repairing waste; and I have seen sick, and not a few either, whose craving for cheese shewed how much it was needed by them.

But, if fresh milk is so valuable a food for the sick, the least change or sourness in it, makes it of all articles, perhaps, the most injurious; diarrhœa is a common result of fresh milk allowed to become at all sour. The nurse therefore ought to exercise her utmost care in this. In large institutions for the sick, even the poorest, the utmost care is exercised. Wenham Lake ice is used for this express purpose every summer, while the private patient, perhaps, never tastes a drop of milk that is not sour, all through the hot weather, so little does the private nurse understand the necessity of such care. Yet, if you consider that the only drop of real nourishment in your patient's tea is the drop of milk, and how much almost all English patients depend upon their tea, you will see the great importance of not depriving your patient of this drop of milk. Buttermilk, a totally different thing, is often very useful, especially in fevers.

Sweet things.
In laying down rules of diet, by the amounts of "solid nutriment" in different kinds of food, it is constantly lost sight of what the patient requires to repair his waste,

what he can take and what he can't. You
cannot diet a patient from a book, you
cannot make up the human body as you
would make up a prescription,—so many
parts "carboniferous," so many parts
"nitrogenous" will constitute a perfect diet
for the patient. The nurse's observation here
will materially assist the doctor—the
patient's "fancies" will materially assist the
nurse. For instance, sugar is one of the most
nutritive of all articles, being pure carbon,
and is particularly recommended in some
books. But the vast majority of all patients in
England, young and old, male and female,
rich and poor, hospital and private, dislike
sweet things,—and while I have never
known a person take to sweets when he was
ill who disliked them when he was well, I
have known many fond of them when in
health, who in sickness would leave off
anything sweet, even to sugar in tea,—sweet
puddings, sweet drinks, are their aversion;
the furred tongue almost always likes what
is sharp or pungent. Scorbutic patients are
an exception, they often crave for
sweetmeats and jams.

Jelly.

Jelly is another article of diet in great favour with nurses and friends of the sick; even if it could be eaten solid, it would not nourish, but it is simply the height of folly to take 1/8 oz. of gelatine and make it into a certain bulk by dissolving it in water and then to give it to the sick, as if the mere bulk represented nourishment. It is now known that jelly does not nourish, that it has a tendency to produce diarrhœa,—and to trust to it to repair the waste of a diseased constitution is simply to starve the sick under the guise of feeding them. If 100 spoonfuls of jelly were given in the course of the day, you would have given one spoonful of gelatine, which spoonful has no nutritive power whatever.

And, nevertheless, gelatine contains a large quantity of nitrogen, which is one of the most powerful elements in nutrition; on the other hand, beef tea may be chosen as an illustration of great nutrient power in sickness, co-existing with a very small amount of solid nitrogenous matter.

Beef tea.
Dr. Christison says that "every one will be

struck with the readiness with which"
certain classes of "patients will often take
diluted meat juice or beef tea repeatedly,
when they refuse all other kinds of food."
This is particularly remarkable in "cases of
gastric fever, in which," he says, "little or
nothing else besides beef tea or diluted meat
juice" has been taken for weeks or even
months, "and yet a pint of beef tea contains
scarcely ¼ oz. of anything but water,"—the
result is so striking that he asks what is its
mode of action? "Not simply nutrient—¼
oz. of the most nutritive material cannot
nearly replace the daily wear and tear of the
tissues in any circumstances. Possibly," he
says, "it belongs to a new denomination of
remedies."

It has been observed that a small quantity
of beef tea, added to other articles of
nutrition augments their power out of all
proportion to the additional amount of solid
matter.

The reason why jelly should be
innutritious and beef tea nutritious to the
sick, is a secret yet undiscovered, but it
clearly shows that careful observation of the

sick is the only clue to the best dietary.

Observation, not chemistry, must decide sick diet.

Chemistry has as yet afforded little insight into the dieting of sick. All that chemistry can tell us is the amount of "carboniferous" or "nitrogenous" elements discoverable in different dietetic articles. It has given us lists of dietetic substances, arranged in the order of their richness in one or other of these principles; but that is all. In the great majority of cases, the stomach of the patient is guided by other principles of selection than merely the amount of carbon or nitrogen in the diet. No doubt, in this as in other things, nature has very definite rules for her guidance, but these rules can only be ascertained by the most careful observation at the bed-side. She there teaches us that living chemistry, the chemistry of reparation, is something different from the chemistry of the laboratory. Organic chemistry is useful, as all knowledge is, when we come face to face with nature; but it by no means follows that we should learn in the laboratory any one of the reparative processes going on in disease.

Again, the nutritive power of milk and of the preparations from milk, is very much undervalued; there is nearly as much nourishment in half a pint of milk as there is in a quarter of a lb. of meat. But this is not the whole question or nearly the whole. The main question is what the patient's stomach can assimilate or derive nourishment from, and of this the patient's stomach is the sole judge. Chemistry cannot tell this. The patient's stomach must be its own chemist. The diet which will keep the healthy man healthy, will kill the sick one. The same beef which is the most nutritive of all meat and which nourishes the healthy man, is the least nourishing of all food to the sick man, whose half-dead stomach can assimilate no part of it, that is, make no food out of it. On a diet of beef tea healthy men on the other hand speedily lose their strength.

Home-made bread.

I have known patients live for many months without touching bread, because they could not eat baker's bread. These were mostly country patients, but not all. Home-made bread or brown bread is a most

important article of diet for many patients.
The use of aperients may be entirely
superseded by it. Oat cake is another.

Sound observation has scarcely yet been
brought to bear on sick diet.

To watch for the opinions, then, which the
patient's stomach gives, rather than to read
"analyses of foods," is the business of all
those who have to settle what the patient is
to eat—perhaps the most important thing to
be provided for him after the air he is to
breathe.

Now the medical man who sees the
patient only once a day or even only once or
twice a week, cannot possibly tell this
without the assistance of the patient himself,
or of those who are in constant observation
on the patient. The utmost the medical man
can tell is whether the patient is weaker or
stronger at this visit than he was at the last
visit. I should therefore say that
incomparably the most important office of
the nurse, after she has taken care of the
patient's air, is to take care to observe the
effect of his food, and report it to the
medical attendant.

It is quite incalculable the good that
would certainly come from such sound and
close observation in this almost neglected
branch of nursing, or the help it would give
to the medical man.

Bulk.

An almost universal error among nurses
is in the bulk of the food and especially the
drinks they offer to their patients. Suppose a
patient ordered 4 oz. brandy during the day,
how is he to take this if you make it into four
pints with diluting it? The same with tea
and beef tea, with arrowroot, milk, &c. You
have not increased the nourishment, you
have not increased the renovating power of
these articles, by increasing their bulk,—you
have very likely diminished both by giving
the patient's digestion more to do, and most
likely of all, the patient will leave half of
what he has been ordered to take, because
he cannot swallow the bulk with which you
have been pleased to invest it. It requires
very nice observation and care (and meets
with hardly any) to determine what will not
be too thick or strong for the patient to take,
while giving him no more than the bulk

which he is able to swallow.

- NOTES ON NURSING: WHAT IT IS, AND WHAT IT IS NOT by FLORENCE NIGHTINGALE. (1859)

Meals for people who are in bed are an emergency of housekeeping. In their preparation, economy should not be exercised unless it is grievously necessary. Sick people are easily annoyed and often have no appetite; sometimes they have even a disgust for food. The necessity then is that their food should be the best, the freshest, the most inviting and the most carefully cooked.

It is also important that food should be really hot or really cold when it is intended to be. Coffee or tea served in a little pot or in a covered pitcher rather than in a cup will be hotter and not spilled over into the saucer. Plates and cups which are to contain hot food should be heated very hot, they will be cool enough for use by the time they have been carried upstairs. If the tray must be carried any distance cover hot food with heated plates and bowls. For butter or ice cream or any food which must be cold to look or taste agreeable, chill the plate on which it is to be served and cover it with a chilled bowl or plate. In hot weather put the butter on a little lettuce leaf, or lay a tiny piece of ice beside it.

The appearance of an invalid's tray is often the cause of appetite or of the lack of it. The linen should always be perfectly fresh, the food in small quantities and daintily arranged. The dishes may well be the daintiest and prettiest in the house, and should be small enough for easy use. A flower or a geranium leaf is a pleasant addition to the tray.

Before bringing a meal to an invalid, go and see that she is comfortable. If one has not an invalid's table, it is well to put a pile of books or boxes on each side of the sick person on which the ends of the tray can rest. It takes strength and nerve to balance something on one's lap when half lying down.

- The Library of Work and Play:

Florence Nightingale

HOUSEKEEPING by ELIZABETH HALE GILMAN (1911)

We cannot leave this book without giving a few simple rules for nursing the sick. Most of our young people, and many old, are ignorant of the commonest principles.

Never wear a rustling dress or creaking shoes in waiting on the sick. Be careful not to shake the bed, or fidget near it, so as to touch, disturb, and needlessly fatigue the invalid. Few noises are more irritating in sickness than noise from the grate. The startling effect of putting on coals may destroy the effect of an opiate. It is better to put them on one by one. In voice and manner be gentle, and in spirit cheerful and hopeful. Do not depress by tears, but control looks, words, and actions. Say nothing in the room, or even outside the door, which you would not wish the sick to hear. Ask questions but rarely, and never occasion a needless effort to gratify your own curiosity. In giving nourishment with a spoon, be careful to raise the bowl of the spoon so as not to drop anything, or annoy the sick person by untidy feeding. Be sure to have cups, spoons, and glasses clean. Make everything as attractive as you can from the nicety and freshness of the dish. Do not allow jellies or rejected dainties to remain in the room. The time may come to any boy or girl when they may desire to watch by a sick bed of a parent or friend, and the above rules may assist them.

If the sick person should take a dislike to you, be not disheartened at it; but if possible resign your place by the bedside. It may be that you were clumsy, and awkward, or over-anxious. It may be only one of those unaccountable fancies which sometimes takes possession of the sufferer, and which it is our duty to treat with care and consideration.

1.—COOKING FOR THE SICK.

Beef tea. Take one pound of beef, without any fat, cut it in very small pieces, and put it in a bottle; cork it and put it into a kettle of water, and boil it until the juice is exhausted; this will do for very sick people who can only take a teaspoonful of nourishment at one time. Take a pound of lean beef, cut it up fine in a quart of cold water, let it boil an hour, then salt it, and put in a pinch of cayenne pepper, strain it, and it is ready for use. This given to a person troubled with sleeplessness (from general debility), about a half cup full just before retiring, will generally enable the patient to sleep.

2.—PORT WINE JELLY.

Take a half pint of port wine, one ounce of isinglass, one ounce of gum arabic, one ounce of loaf sugar; let it simmer for a quarter of an hour, stirring it till the gum and isinglass are dissolved, then pour it into a mould. When cold it will be quite stiff.

3.—TOAST WATER.

Brown thoroughly, but not burn to a cinder, a small slice of bread; put it into a pitcher, and pour over it a quart of water which has been boiled and cooled; after two hours pour off the water; a small piece of orange or lemon peel put into the pitcher with the bread improves it.

4.—TO PREPARE RENNET WHEY.

Get a rennet, such as is used for cheeses. Then take a piece two inches square, or a little larger, rinse it first in cold water, then pour on to it two table-spoonfuls of hot water, and let it stand a half hour in a warm place. Take three pints of milk, and heat it blood warm. Then pour in both the rennet and water, and stir it in well. Cover and let it stand in a warm place, to keep the milk of an even temperature; it must not be moved until it turns to a curd; then cut up the curd with a spoon and strain it, and boil up the whey once. It is then ready for use. If in an hour it does not turn to a curd, take out the rennet, and put in some more freshly prepared. It will then surely curd.

- Home Arts FOR OLD AND YOUNG. By MRS. CAROLINE L. SMITH. (1837)

CHAPTER FIVE

"Long live the sisters,"

Miss Nightingale too, had read the letter in the Times, and was thinking over it in her home in the country. Before Mr. Herbert's letter reached her, she wrote to him of her own accord offering her services to go as nurse to the hospitals at Scutari. The moment had come for which unconsciously she had been long preparing, and she was ready for the work which came to her. Her letter crossed Mr. Herbert's. It was written on October 15, 1854, and immediately it was announced in the Times that Miss Nightingale had been appointed Superintendent of Nurses at Scutari. She at once set to work to collect the band of thirty-eight nurses whom she was to take out with her. There were a few Institutions in existence for training nurses, and to these Miss Nightingale appealed for volunteers. Twenty-four of those she took out came from such places. Six days after she had made her offer to go, she was ready to start with her band complete. They crossed the Channel to Boulogne, where the people had heard of their coming; the fishwives turned out to meet them, and insisted on carrying their bags from the boat to the train. They, too, were interested in the war where English and French soldiers were fighting side by side, and as they walked with them they begged the nurses to take care of any of their dear ones should they meet them. With tears and warm shakes of the hand they bade farewell to them, crying, "Long live the sisters," as the train carried them away.

Prayer for the Wounded.

Lord God, our Heavenly Father! We implore Thy eternal compassion for all who are this day wounded, suffering, or dying. Be Thou nigh unto them in their affliction. Comfort

them with Thy grace and
with the hopeful assurance,
that, though kindred and
friends be far away, Thou
art ever present and
hearest even the faintest
sight of all who seek Thy
succor. If it be Thy
pleasure, restore to them
their former health and
vigor. Help them to bear
their pains without
murmuring against Thy
grace. Give them patience
and strength and faith in
Thee. May they rest
assured, that Thou wilt
never leave nor forsake
them. Deliver them from the
assaults of the enemies of
their souls. O God and
Father in heaven, bless
them and all of us, and may
we ever seek those things
that are acceptable to Thy
sight. Forgive us our sins,
not because of any merit or
worthiness in us, but
solely because Thou art
merciful for Christ's sake.
And to Thee, the Father,
Son, and Holy Ghost, be
glory and honor forever.
Amen.

On November 4th, Miss Nightingale and her nurses reached Scutari, where the poor men in hospital had heard of their coming, but could not believe the good news. One man cried when he saw them, exclaiming, "I can't help it when I see them. Only think of English women coming out here to nurse us! It seems so homelike and comfortable." It was a terrible state of things that Miss Nightingale found in the hospitals. The filth, misery, and disorder were indescribable. In the long corridors the wounded men lay crowded together; many of them had not even had their wounds dressed, nor their broken limbs set. There were no vessels for water, no towels or soap, no hospital clothes. The men lay in their uniforms, stiff with blood. The beds were reeking with infection, and rats and vermin of every kind swarmed over them. There was no time to plan reforms or to bring any order into the hospitals before more wounded from the battle of Inkermann arrived in terrible numbers, only twenty-four hours after Miss Nightingale had come. Her courage rose to the occasion, terrible though it was, and

inspired her companions. Whilst they all
worked without ceasing to do what they
could to help the worst suffering, she, in the
midst of all her labours, thought out what
could be done to bring order into the awful
confusion. She had to see that proper
supplies of all the things needed for the
comfort of the soldiers were sent out from
England, and to make arrangements for the
distribution of the stores when they arrived.
Her energy and her disregard of some of the
rules laid down by the military authorities
about the distribution of the stores made
some people very angry, and there was a
good deal of grumbling at what they
considered her unnecessary haste and her
interference. But Miss Nightingale cared for
nothing so long as she could do the task for
which she had been sent out. She set up a
kitchen where food could be cooked for the
sick and wounded, and a laundry where
their clothes could be washed and
disinfected. She wrote to England clear
accounts of the state of things she had
found, without any grumbling, but pointed
out what had to be done for the proper care
of the men. Opposition to her ways
disappeared as it became clear how

admirable were the results of her work. She won the orderlies to work with the utmost patience and devotion under the direction of the lady nurses; so that she could say that not one of them failed her in obedience, thoughtful attention, and considerate delicacy. They were rough, ignorant men, but in the midst of scenes of loathsome disease and death they showed to Miss Nightingale and her nurses the most courteous chivalry and constant gentleness, and she never heard from them a word that could shock her.

Florence Nightingale at Scutari—A Mission of Mercy.
(After the Picture by Jerry Barrett.)

CHAPTER SIX

Indications of Sickness

Temperature.
—Bodily heat is produced by slow burning of food materials, which goes on for the most part in actively working muscles and glands. Heat thus generated is distributed by the blood to all parts of the body, but the surface of the body is generally cooler than the interior. In health the body temperature varies only a few degrees, no matter how much the temperature of its surroundings varies; consequently a temperature is abnormal if it is higher or lower than the usual temperature of a healthy person.

Florence Nightingale

Fig. 10.—

Clinical Thermometer.

The temperature is taken by means of a
clinical thermometer placed either in the
mouth, the rectum, or the armpit (axilla).

To take the mouth temperature, first wash
the thermometer, using cold water and
absorbent cotton or clean soft cloth. Next
shake it until the mercury thread registers
96° or below. It is well before purchasing a
thermometer to see whether it can be shaken
down easily. Next place the thermometer in
the patient's mouth, with its bulb under his
tongue; he must then keep his lips closed
until it is removed. Leave the thermometer
in his mouth for two minutes. Then remove
the thermometer, read the temperature and
record the result. Clean the thermometer at
once, using first cold water and soap, and
then alcohol, 70%.

The mouth temperature of a healthy
person is about 98.6° F. This statement holds
true if the person has been sitting with his
mouth shut for a little while before his
temperature is taken; but a hot bath,
breathing through the mouth, eating or

drinking, and so forth may cause marked temporary changes.

The temperature in the rectum generally varies less than the temperature in the mouth unless it is taken when the rectum contains fecal matter. The temperature should be taken by rectum in babies and young children, restless, drowsy, or delirious patients, patients who cannot be trusted to keep the thermometer under the tongue, mouth breathers, and in any patients who have difficulty in keeping the mouth shut. The temperature is normally about half a degree higher in the rectum than in the mouth.

In order to take a temperature by rectum, adults generally find it more convenient to lie on the side and prefer, if they are able, to insert and hold the thermometer themselves; but the attendant should be certain that they can do so without breaking the thermometer. Rectal thermometers should be lubricated with oil or vaseline before using; they should be inserted about two inches, left in three minutes, and cleansed in the same way as the mouth thermometer. A

thermometer used to take rectal
temperatures should never be used in the
mouth.

In taking the temperature of a baby place
him on his back, hold him firmly with his
legs elevated, and carefully insert the bulb of
the thermometer, well oiled, for about one
inch. Keep the child quiet, and hold the
thermometer in place three minutes. Great
importance should not be attached to a
slight fever of short duration. The
temperature of a child is much more easily
affected by slight causes than that of an
adult, and rectal temperatures between 97.5°
and 100.5° should not cause anxiety unless
continued.

Temperatures taken in the axilla are less
accurate than those taken by mouth or
rectum. Consequently the method is less
often used. The axilla should first be wiped;
then the thermometer should be inserted
and held for 5 minutes by pressing the arm
tightly against the chest wall. The
temperature in the axilla is normally about
half a degree lower than in the mouth.

The temperature varies somewhat according to the time of day. It is not unusual for the mouth temperature of persons who are entirely healthy to be as low as 97° in the early morning, or as high as 99° in the late afternoon, and probably most people's temperatures vary as much as a degree during the twenty-four hours. Even greater variations that are not long continued have little if any significance in people who feel well.

Decided variations either above or below normal are highly important symptoms. A temperature below 98° is called subnormal, and one above 99.5° is called fever. The number of degrees of fever does not necessarily bear a direct relation to the severity of an illness. Thus, it does not follow that one person is twice as sick as another, because his temperature is twice as many degrees above normal. All symptoms, including variations in temperature, must be considered in connection with one another, and it is generally impossible to state the significance of any one symptom taken by itself.

The temperature should be taken once or twice a day as a matter of routine in almost every form of illness, and oftener when the patient's condition requires it. Also it should be taken as a matter of routine whenever there is indication of beginning sickness; especially when there is headache, pain, sore throat, coated tongue, cough or cold, chill, vomiting, diarrhœa, or rash. It is not a good plan to take one's own temperature oftener than necessary, or indeed anyone's; certainly not a baby's, since frequent use of the thermometer may irritate the rectum.

Pulse.
—Each time the heart beats, blood is forced out from the heart into the arteries, thus causing an expansion of the arterial walls. This expansion, called the pulse, can be felt in some places where arteries lie close to the surface of the body. The character of the pulse beat and its rate, or the number of times the beat occurs each minute, give information about the heart and blood vessels; taken together they are perhaps more important than any other one symptom.

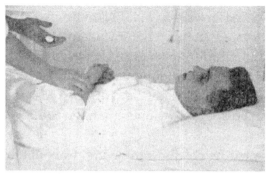

Taking the pulse at the wrist. Note the position of arm.

(From "Elementary Nursing Procedures," California State Board of Health.)

The pulse rate varies much more than the temperature. It differs in different individuals and at different ages, and it often shows great temporary changes, especially during exercise or eating, or as a result of excitement, fear, or other emotion. Definite statements in regard to normal pulse rates are hard to make, because different individuals though in perfect health show marked variations; we generally say, however, that the pulse rate of a normal man at rest is about 72 a minute, and that of a normal woman is about 80 a minute. At birth the pulse is quickest; it may then be from 124 to 144. From the 6th to the 12th month it may be from 105 to 115 a minute, and from 90 to 105 between the 2d and 6th years. About the time of puberty it reaches the adult rate, and during old age it may be decidedly slower than the adult rate.

What we chiefly want to know about the pulse is

1. Its rate, or number of beats per minute,

2. Its force,—whether weak or strong,

3. Its rhythm,—whether regular or irregular.

Much practice is necessary before the pulse rate can be counted with any degree of accuracy, and wide experience with both normal and abnormal pulses is required in order to judge its strength, rhythm, or other characteristics.

The pulse may be felt most conveniently on the thumb side of the front of the wrist. The pulse should be counted while the patient is lying down, and the watch used must have a second hand. To count the pulse, one should place two or three fingers (not the thumb) on the patient's wrist, and after the pulse has been felt distinctly for a few beats, the exact time by the second hand of the watch should be noticed and the counting begun immediately. It is generally best to count for half a minute, multiply the result by two to get the rate for a whole minute, and then to repeat for another half minute. The two results should agree within two beats, if the patient is quiet. A greater variation than two beats may mean that the pulse rate is varying, but when it is counted by inexperienced persons the apparent difference is generally the result of inaccurate counting, and it may be necessary to count two or three times more. The force of the pulse varies also in different individuals; it is, however, important to notice when it grows stronger or weaker in the same person. Normally the pulse-beat is regular like the ticking of a clock; it is called irregular if a few rapid or slow beats are followed by others of a different rate. During sickness the pulse should be counted whenever the temperature is taken, or oftener; and the result should be written down at once. The pulse of a sick person often shows changes both in rate and character; these changes are generally important and should be noticed.

Respiration.

—Variations in the rate and character of respiration or breathing should be noticed. The normal rate of respiration for an adult at rest is 16 to 20 each minute, but it may be much faster, especially during muscular exercise. In babies the rate is about 30 to 35 a minute, and 20 to 25 in little children. The respirations, especially of babies, can best be counted during sleep by placing the hand lightly on the chest or abdomen. Since the respiration rate is partly under a person's control, it is almost sure to alter if the patient knows it is being counted; hence when the patient is awake it is better to keep one's fingers on his wrist, to place his hand upon his chest, and then to count the rise and fall of the chest while apparently counting the pulse. Sometimes it is possible to count the respirations merely by watching the rise and fall of the nightgown or bed clothes. The respiration is usually counted for a full minute. A watch with a second hand must be used, and the result should be recorded immediately.

In certain forms of sickness breathing may become rapid, especially if the lungs or air passages are affected. In addition to the rate anything unusual about the breathing should be noticed whether it seems difficult or painful; if noisy, whether the sound is like snoring, or wheezing, or sighing, and so on.

General Appearance.

—Any unusual expression of the face should be noted; whether it is drawn, pinched, anxious, excited, or dull and stupid; and also, whether the face is thin, swollen, or puffy under the eyes. The condition and appearance of the skin are significant: the skin may be dry, moist and clammy, hot or cold; its color, and the color of the face especially, may be flushed or pale or slightly yellow or blue. A bluish tinge about the nose, tips of the fingers, or the feet should be specially noticed. Reddened or discolored areas on any part of the body may be important, and also eruptions, rashes, swellings, or sores. It should be noticed whether the abdomen is normal or whether it is distended and hard.

Strength or weakness is indicated to some extent by the way the patient moves, and by his ability to walk, stand, sit, hold up his head, feed himself, or turn in bed without assistance. The position he habitually takes is sometimes significant; in heart affections, for instance, he may be unable to lie down, in pleurisy he ordinarily lies on the affected side, and during abdominal pain he generally draws the knees up.

Special Senses.

—The special senses are frequently disturbed in sickness. The eyes may be blood-shot; the patient may be over-sensitive to light, or see spots floating before the eyes, or he may be unable to see at all. The pupils of the eyes may be unusually large or small, or one may be large while the other is small. Swelling, redness, or discharge from the eyes should be noticed. Hearing and touch and smell may be impaired; or they may be abnormally acute, and cause real suffering. Taste may be impaired, especially when the nose is affected or when the mouth is not clean. Discharge from the nose or ears should be reported. Not only discharge, but also trouble of any kind, such as pain,

71

tenderness, or swelling, is important if situated in or near the ears.

The voice is often much altered in sickness. It may be weak, hoarse, or whispered. Speech may be clear or thick, or the ability to speak may be entirely lost; in extreme weakness speaking is generally difficult, and may be impossible. Moaning, groaning, and other unusual sounds should be noted. A loud, sharp cry at night with or without waking, if a repeated occurrence, may be an early symptom of some diseases of children.

The tongue in health is red and moist; when extended it is somewhat pointed and can be held steadily. In sickness it may be cracked, dry and parched, or if the patient is not properly cared for, it may be covered with white, yellow, or brown coating; in many exhausting illnesses it is flabby and trembling. In scarlet fever the tongue is often a vivid red color, and is then called strawberry tongue. The odor of the breath may be foul from decay or neglect of the teeth, from indigestion, constipation, nasal catarrh, or special diseases.

The throat and tonsils are sometimes red and swollen as in simple sore throat; or they may be covered by white patches.

The gums may be swollen, tender, or bleeding. A collection of sticky brownish material may appear on the teeth and gums of neglected patients.

Cough when present may be: dry, or accompanied by expectoration; painful, frequent, loud, or whooping; and worse by day or by night. The sputum may be yellow, white, gray, rusty, blood-streaked, dark, or frothy. The amount of sputum should be noticed as well as its appearance.

Appetite or absence of appetite should be noted, and also the amount of food actually eaten by a patient; the amount eaten is frequently not the same as the amount carried to him on a tray.

If vomiting occurs, the color, consistency, amount, and general appearance of the vomitus should be noted; if its appearance is unusual the vomitus should be saved for the doctor's inspection.

Excretions.

—The number of bowel movements is important, and also their character. The consistency of the feces may be hard, soft or fluid; their color may be any shade of brown, yellow or green, from black to clay color. They should be saved for the doctor to see if appearance or odor is unusual.

The urine in health is clear, amber colored, and slightly acid. From 30 to 50 ounces should be excreted in 24 hours; the amount varies, however, especially according to the amount of fluid taken. It is important to notice whether the urine is scanty or greatly increased in amount, dark or pale, clear or cloudy, and whether sediment is deposited after standing. It is essential that urine should be voided in sufficient amount; the necessity for watching its quantity is frequently overlooked in the home care of the sick. Frequency of urination should also be noted. Inability to urinate, particularly where the urine has previously been scanty, is serious if continued; it should be reported to the doctor without delay. Inability to control the bladder and bowels are also symptoms to be reported.

Loss of weight is significant in both adults and children, and failure of babies and children to gain in weight is a danger signal.

Sleep.

—The number of hours a patient sleeps should be noticed and recorded as accurately as possible. The word of the patient on this subject is not sufficient evidence. Character of sleep should also be noted, whether it is quiet or restless, and whether the patient sleeps lightly or is difficult to arouse.

Mental Conditions.—It is important to watch carefully the mental condition of a patient; whether, for example, he is normal, or depressed, irritable, restless, apathetic, dull, excited, wandering, delirious, or unconscious. Hasty judgment of mental conditions should be avoided, but close attention to them is necessary.

- AMERICAN RED CROSS TEXT-BOOK ON HOME CARE OF THE SICK by JANE A. DELANO, R. N. (1918)

CHAPTER SEVEN

The Lady of the Lamp

The gratitude and devotion of the patients to her knew no bounds. At nights she used to pass through the long corridors, and the endless wards—there were four miles of wards in the hospital—carrying a little lamp in her hand, so as to see that all was well, and from this the patients learnt to call her "the lady of the lamp." They felt that she was their good angel, and one of them said afterwards, describing the comfort it was even to see her pass, "She would speak to one and another, and nod and smile to many more, but she could not do it to all for we lay there by hundreds; but we would kiss her shadow as it fell, and lay our heads on the pillow again content."

Huddled together in two or three damp rooms in the basement of the hospital, Miss Nightingale found a great number of poor women, the wives of the soldiers, with their babies, living in the utmost misery and discomfort. She did not rest till she had arranged better quarters for them. Some ladies were found to befriend them. Those whose husbands had been killed in the war were sent back to England, many were given work in the laundry which Miss Nightingale had started, and a school was opened for the children.

Florence Nightingale in one of the Wards of the Hospital at Scutari.

When the winter came on, the sufferings

of the soldiers increased. The army was
engaged in the siege of Sevastopol, and Miss
Nightingale described the sufferings
endured by the soldiers there in a letter to a
friend: "Fancy working five nights out of
seven in the trenches! Fancy being thirty-six
hours in them at a stretch, with no food but
raw salt pork sprinkled with sugar, rum,
and biscuit; nothing hot ... fancy through all
this the army preserving their courage and
patience as they have done. There is
something sublime in the spectacle." The
hospitals were crowded with men brought
in ill from the results of this exposure. Early
in 1855 fifty more trained nurses were sent
out from England, and they came in time to
help in a terrible outbreak of cholera which
filled the hospital with new patients, most of
whom died after a few hours' suffering.
Frost-bitten men were brought in too from
Sevastopol, and of all these sufferers at least
half died in spite of the care of the nurses.
Again and again it was Miss Nightingale
who comforted the dying and received from
them the last message to be sent to the dear
ones at home. She wrote down their words
and took care of their watches or other
possessions which they wished to send

home.

Prayers for the Dying. (St. Paul's Prayer)

"The time of my departure is at hand. I have fought a good fight, I have finished my course, I have kept the faith: henceforth there is laid up for me a crown of righteousness, which the Lord, the righteous judge, shall give me at that day: not to me only, but to all of them also that love His appearing." 2 Tim. 4:6-8.

* * *

O Lord, on Thy cross Thou didst cry, "Father, into Thy hands I commend My Spirit!" I, too, commend my spirit into Thy hands now when my end is near. Thou hast redeemed me, O faithful God. Amen.

* * *

Lord Almighty God, Heavenly Father! My time has come to an end, my life is slowly

ebbing away. Be Thou with
me. O Lord, I suffer much
and Thou only canst help
me. Be Thou my succor, and
shorten and soften my pain.
Darkness comes over me and
I cry for comfort and
strength. Have mercy upon
me. Take my soul under Thy
protecting wing, that I
perish not. Take my sins
from me, and blot all my
guilt; for Christ's sake,
my Savior and my Lord.
Amen.

Abide with me! fast falls
the eventide.

The darkness deepens: Lord,
with me abide!

When other helpers fail and
comforts flee,

Help of the helpless, O
abide with me!

Hold Thou Thy cross before
my closing eyes,

Shine through the gloom,
and point me to the skies:

Florence Nightingale

Heaven's morning breaks,
and earth's vain shadows
flee:

In life, in death, O Lord,
abide with me!

CHAPTER EIGHT

Notes on Nursing: Health of Houses

HEALTH OF HOUSES.

Health of houses. Five points essential.

There are five essential points in securing the health of houses:—

Pure air.
Pure water.
Efficient drainage.
Cleanliness.
Light.

Without these, no house can be healthy. And it will be unhealthy just in proportion as they are deficient.

Pure air.

1. To have pure air, your house must be so

constructed as that the outer atmosphere shall find its way with ease to every corner of it. House architects hardly ever consider this. The object in building a house is to obtain the largest interest for the money, not to save doctors' bills to the tenants. But, if tenants should ever become so wise as to refuse to occupy unhealthily constructed houses, and if Insurance Companies should ever come to understand their interest so thoroughly as to pay a Sanitary Surveyor to look after the houses where their clients live, speculative architects would speedily be brought to their senses. As it is, they build what pays best. And there are always people foolish enough to take the houses they build. And if in the course of time the families die off, as is so often the case, nobody ever thinks of blaming any but Providence for the result. Ill-informed medical men aid in sustaining the delusion, by laying the blame on "current contagions." Badly constructed houses do for the healthy what badly constructed hospitals do for the sick. Once insure that the air in a house is stagnant, and sickness is certain to follow.

Pure water.

2. Pure water is more generally introduced into houses than it used to be, thanks to the exertions of the sanitary reformers. Within the last few years, a large part of London was in the daily habit of using water polluted by the drainage of its sewers and water closets. This has happily been remedied. But, in many parts of the country, well water of a very impure kind is used for domestic purposes. And when epidemic disease shows itself, persons using such water are almost sure to suffer.

Drainage.

3. It would be curious to ascertain by inspection, how many houses in London are really well drained. Many people would say, surely all or most of them. But many people have no idea in what good drainage consists. They think that a sewer in the street, and a pipe leading to it from the house is good drainage. All the while the sewer may be nothing but a laboratory from which epidemic disease and ill health is being distilled into the house. No house with any untrapped drain pipe communicating immediately with a sewer, whether it be from water closet, sink, or

gully-grate, can ever be healthy. An untrapped sink may at any time spread fever or pyæmia among the inmates of a palace.

Sinks.

The ordinary oblong sink is an abomination. That great surface of stone, which is always left wet, is always exhaling into the air. I have known whole houses and hospitals smell of the sink. I have met just as strong a stream of sewer air coming up the back staircase of a grand London house from the sink, as I have ever met at Scutari; and I have seen the rooms in that house all ventilated by the open doors, and the passages all unventilated by the closed windows, in order that as much of the sewer air as possible might be conducted into and retained in the bed-rooms. It is wonderful.

Another great evil in house construction is carrying drains underneath the house. Such drains are never safe. All house drains should begin and end outside the walls. Many people will readily admit, as a theory, the importance of these things. But how few are there who can intelligently trace disease in their households to such causes! Is it not a fact, that when scarlet fever, measles, or small-pox appear among the children, the very first thought which occurs is, "where" the children can have "caught" the disease? And the parents immediately run over in their minds all the families with whom they may have been. They never think of looking at home for the source of the mischief. If a neighbour's child is seized with small pox, the first question which occurs is whether it had been vaccinated. No one would undervalue vaccination; but it becomes of doubtful benefit to society when it leads people to look abroad for the source of evils which exist at home.

Cleanliness.

4. Without cleanliness, within and without your house, ventilation is comparatively useless. In certain foul districts of London, poor people used to object to open their windows and doors because of the foul smells that came in. Rich people like to have their stables and dunghill near their houses. But does it ever occur to them that with many arrangements of this kind it would be safer to keep the windows shut than open?

You cannot have the air of the house pure with dung heaps under the windows. These are common all over London. And yet people are surprised that their children, brought up in large "well-aired" nurseries and bed-rooms suffer from children's epidemics. If they studied Nature's laws in the matter of children's health, they would not be so surprised.

There are other ways of having filth inside a house besides having dirt in heaps. Old papered walls of years' standing, dirty carpets, uncleansed furniture, are just as ready sources of impurity to the air as if there were a dung-heap in the basement. People are so unaccustomed from education and habits to consider how to make a home healthy, that they either never think of it at all, and take every disease as a matter of course, to be "resigned to" when it comes "as from the hand of Providence;" or if they ever entertain the idea of preserving the health of their household as a duty, they are very apt to commit all kinds of "negligences and ignorances" in performing it.

Light.

5. A dark house is always an unhealthy house, always an ill-aired house, always a dirty house. Want of light stops growth, and promotes scrofula, rickets, &c., among the children.

People lose their health in a dark house, and if they get ill they cannot get well again in it. More will be said about this farther on.

Three common errors in managing the health of houses.

Three out of many "negligences and ignorances" in managing the health of houses generally, I will here mention as specimens—1. That the female head in charge of any building does not think it necessary to visit every hole and corner of it every day. How can she expect those who are under her to be more careful to maintain her house in a healthy condition than she who is in charge of it?—2. That it is not considered essential to air, to sun, and to clean rooms while uninhabited; which is simply ignoring the first elementary notion of sanitary things, and laying the ground ready for all kinds of diseases.—3. That the window, and one window, is considered

enough to air a room. Have you never
observed that any room without a fire-place
is always close? And, if you have a fire-
place, would you cram it up not only with a
chimney-board, but perhaps with a great
wisp of brown paper, in the throat of the
chimney—to prevent the soot from coming
down, you say? If your chimney is foul,
sweep it; but don't expect that you can ever
air a room with only one aperture; don't
suppose that to shut up a room is the way to
keep it clean. It is the best way to foul the
room and all that is in it. Don't imagine that
if you, who are in charge, don't look to all
these things yourself, those under you will
be more careful than you are. It appears as if
the part of a mistress now is to complain of
her servants, and to accept their excuses—
not to show them how there need be neither
complaints made nor excuses.

Head in charge must see to House
Hygiene, not do it herself.

But again, to look to all these things
yourself does not mean to do them yourself.
"I always open the windows," the head in
charge often says. If you do it, it is by so
much the better, certainly, than if it were not

done at all. But can you not insure that it is done when not done by yourself? Can you insure that it is not undone when your back is turned? This is what being "in charge" means. And a very important meaning it is, too. The former only implies that just what you can do with your own hands is done. The latter that what ought to be done is always done.

Does God think of these things so seriously?

And now, you think these things trifles, or at least exaggerated. But what you "think" or what I "think" matters little. Let us see what God thinks of them. God always justifies His ways. While we are thinking, He has been teaching. I have known cases of hospital pyæmia quite as severe in handsome private houses as in any of the worst hospitals, and from the same cause, viz., foul air. Yet nobody learnt the lesson. Nobody learnt anything at all from it. They went on thinking—thinking that the sufferer had scratched his thumb, or that it was singular that "all the servants" had "whitlows," or that something was "much about this year; there is always sickness in our house." This is a favourite mode of thought—leading not to inquire what is the uniform cause of these general "whitlows," but to stifle all inquiry. In what sense is "sickness" being "always there," a justification of its being "there" at all?

How does He carry out His laws?
I will tell you what was the cause of this hospital pyæmia being in that large private house. It was that the sewer air from an ill-placed sink was carefully conducted into all the rooms by sedulously opening all the doors; and closing all the passage windows. It was that the slops were emptied into the foot pans;—it was that the utensils were never properly rinsed;—it was that the chamber crockery was rinsed with dirty water;—it was that the beds were never properly shaken, aired, picked to pieces, or changed. It was that the carpets and curtains were always musty;—it was that the furniture was always dusty; it was that the papered walls were saturated with dirt;—it was that the floors were never cleaned;—it was that the uninhabited rooms were never sunned, or cleaned, or aired;—it was that the cupboards were always reservoirs of foul

air;—it was that the windows were always tight shut up at night;—it was that no window was ever systematically opened, even in the day, or that the right window was not opened. A person gasping for air might open a window for himself. But the servants were not taught to open the windows, to shut the doors; or they opened the windows upon a dank well between high walls, not upon the airier court; or they opened the room doors into the unaired halls and passages, by way of airing the rooms. Now all this is not fancy, but fact. How does He teach His laws?In that handsome house I have known in one summer three cases of hospital pyæmia, one of phlebitis, two of consumptive cough: all the immediate products of foul air. When, in temperate climates, a house is more unhealthy in summer than in winter, it is a certain sign of something wrong. Yet nobody learns the lesson. Yes, God always justifies His ways. He is teaching while you are not learning. This poor body loses his finger, that one loses his life. And all from the most easily preventible causes.

BED AND BEDDING.

Feverishness a symptom of bedding.

A few words upon bedsteads and bedding; and principally as regards patients who are entirely, or almost entirely, confined to bed.

Feverishness is generally supposed to be a symptom of fever—in nine cases out of ten it is a symptom of bedding. The patient has had re-introduced into the body the emanations from himself which day after day and week after week saturate his unaired bedding. How can it be otherwise? Look at the ordinary bed in which a patient lies.

Uncleanliness of ordinary bedding.

If I were looking out for an example in order to show what not to do, I should take the specimen of an ordinary bed in a private house: a wooden bedstead, two or even three mattresses piled up to above the height of a table; a vallance attached to the frame— nothing but a miracle could ever thoroughly dry or air such a bed and bedding. The patient must inevitably alternate between cold damp after his bed is made, and warm damp before, both saturated with organic matter, and this from the time the mattresses are put under him till the time they are picked to pieces, if this is ever done.

Air your dirty sheets, not only your clean ones.

If you consider that an adult in health exhales by the lungs and skin in the twenty-four hours three pints at least of moisture, loaded with organic matter ready to enter into putrefaction; that in sickness the quantity is often greatly increased, the quality is always more noxious—just ask yourself next where does all this moisture go to? Chiefly into the bedding, because it cannot go anywhere else. And it stays there; because, except perhaps a weekly change of sheets, scarcely any other airing is attempted. A nurse will be careful to fidgetiness about airing the clean sheets from clean damp, but airing the dirty sheets from noxious damp will never even occur to her. Besides this, the most dangerous effluvia we know of are from the excreta of the sick—these are placed, at least temporarily, where they must throw their effluvia into the under side of the bed, and the space under the bed is never aired; it cannot be, with our arrangements. Must not such a bed be always saturated, and be always the means of re-introducing into the system of the unfortunate patient who lies in it, that excrementitious matter to eliminate which from the body nature had expressly appointed the disease?

My heart always sinks within me when I hear the good house-wife, of every class, say, "I assure you the bed has been well slept in," and I can only hope it is not true. What? is the bed already saturated with somebody else's damp before my patient comes to exhale into it his own damp? Has it not had a single chance to be aired? No, not one. "It has been slept in every night."

Iron spring bedstead the best.

The only way of really nursing a real patient is to have an iron bedstead, with rheocline springs, which are permeable by the air up to the very mattress (no vallance, of course), the mattress to be a thin hair one; the bed to be not above 3½ feet wide.Comfort and cleanliness of two beds. If the patient be entirely confined to his bed, there should be two such bedsteads; each bed to be "made" with mattress, sheets, blankets, &c., complete—the patient to pass twelve hours in each bed; on no account to carry his sheets with him. The whole of the bedding to be hung up to air for each intermediate twelve hours. Of course there are many cases where this cannot be done at all—many more where only an approach to it can be made. I am indicating the ideal of nursing, and what I have actually had done. But about the kind of bedstead there can be no doubt, whether there be one or two provided.

Bed not to be too wide.

There is a prejudice in favour of a wide bed—I believe it to be a prejudice. All the refreshment of moving a patient from one side to the other of his bed is far more effectually secured by putting him into a fresh bed; and a patient who is really very ill does not stray far in bed. But it is said there is no room to put a tray down on a narrow bed. No good nurse will ever put a tray on a bed at all. If the patient can turn on his side, he will eat more comfortably from a bed-side table; and on no account whatever should a bed ever be higher than a sofa.

Otherwise the patient feels himself "out of humanity's reach"; he can get at nothing for himself: he can move nothing for himself. If the patient cannot turn, a table over the bed is a better thing. I need hardly say that a patient's bed should never have its side against the wall. The nurse must be able to get easily to both sides the bed, and to reach easily every part of the patient without stretching—a thing impossible if the bed be either too wide or too high.

Bed not to be too high.

When I see a patient in a room nine or ten feet high upon a bed between four and five feet high, with his head, when he is sitting up in bed, actually within two or three feet of the ceiling, I ask myself, is this expressly planned to produce that peculiarly distressing feeling common to the sick, viz., as if the walls and ceiling were closing in upon them, and they becoming sandwiches between floor and ceiling, which imagination is not, indeed, here so far from the truth? If, over and above this, the window stops short of the ceiling, then the patient's head may literally be raised above the stratum of fresh air, even when the

window is open. Can human perversity any
farther go, in unmaking the process of
restoration which God has made? The fact
is, that the heads of sleepers or of sick
should never be higher than the throat of the
chimney, which ensures their being in the
current of best air. And we will not suppose
it possible that you have closed your
chimney with a chimney-board.

If a bed is higher than a sofa, the
difference of the fatigue of getting in and out
of bed will just make the difference, very
often, to the patient (who can get in and out
of bed at all) of being able to take a few
minutes' exercise, either in the open air or in
another room. It is so very odd that people
never think of this, or of how many more
times a patient who is in bed for the twenty-
four hours is obliged to get in and out of bed
than they are, who only, it is to be hoped,
get into bed once and out of bed once during
the twenty-four hours.

Nor in a dark place.
A patient's bed should always be in the
lightest spot in the room; and he should be
able to see out of window.

Nor a four poster with curtains.

I need scarcely say that the old four-post bed with curtains is utterly inadmissible, whether for sick or well. Hospital bedsteads are in many respects very much less objectionable than private ones.

Scrofula often a result of disposition of bedclothes.

There is reason to believe that not a few of the apparently unaccountable cases of scrofula among children proceed from the habit of sleeping with the head under the bed clothes, and so inhaling air already breathed, which is farther contaminated by exhalations from the skin. Patients are sometimes given to a similar habit, and it often happens that the bed clothes are so disposed that the patient must necessarily breathe air more or less contaminated by exhalations from his skin. A good nurse will be careful to attend to this. It is an important part, so to speak, of ventilation.

Bed sores.

It may be worth while to remark, that where there is any danger of bed-sores a blanket should never be placed under the patient. It retains damp and acts like a poultice.

Heavy and impervious bedclothes.

Never use anything but light Witney blankets as bed covering for the sick. The heavy cotton impervious counterpane is bad, for the very reason that it keeps in the emanations from the sick person, while the blanket allows them to pass through. Weak patients are invariably distressed by a great weight of bed-clothes, which often prevents their getting any sound sleep whatever.

Note.—One word about pillows.

Every weak patient, be his illness what it may, suffers more or less from difficulty in breathing. To take the weight of the body off the poor chest, which is hardly up to its work as it is, ought therefore to be the object of the nurse in arranging his pillows. Now what does she do and what are the consequences? She piles the pillows one a-top of the other like a wall of bricks. The head is thrown upon the chest. And the shoulders are pushed forward, so as not to allow the lungs room to expand. The pillows, in fact, lean upon the patient, not the patient upon the pillows. It is impossible to give a rule for this, because it must vary with the figure of the patient. And tall patients suffer much more than short ones, because of the drag of the long limbs upon the waist. But the object is to support, with the pillows, the back below the breathing apparatus, to allow the shoulders room to fall back, and to support the head, without throwing it forward. The suffering of dying patients is immensely increased by neglect of these points. And many an invalid, too weak to drag about his pillows himself, slips his book or anything at hand behind the lower part of his back to support it.

- NOTES ON NURSING: WHAT IT IS, AND WHAT IT IS NOT by FLORENCE NIGHTINGALE. (1859)

CHAPTER NINE

Crimean fever

The hearts of people in England were stirred by all they heard of the sufferings of the soldiers and of the devotion of the nurses. Supplies of every kind were sent out in great quantities, and all that was needed was that their use should be wisely organised. Miss Nightingale was much helped by the arrival of M. Soyer, the famous French cook, who came out at his own expense to organise the cooking in the hospitals. He introduced new stoves and many reforms in the kitchens, and was a most devoted admirer of the Lady-in-Chief, as Miss Nightingale was called.

After six months' work at Scutari, Miss

Nightingale set out to visit the hospitals in
the Crimea itself. M. Soyer and several of
her nurses went with her. She rode to the
camp near Balaclava, where she could hear
the thunder of the guns which besieged
Sevastopol. As she passed through the
camp, some of the men who had been her
patients at Scutari recognised her, and
greeted her with a hearty cheer. The
hundreds of sick in the field hospital were
delighted to receive a visit from the lady of
whom they had heard so much. Afterwards
she rode right up into the trenches outside
Sevastopol, so that the sentry was alarmed
at her daring. Next day she visited another
hospital at Balaclava and left some of her
nurses to work there. She was on board the
ship which was to take her back to Scutari,
when she was suddenly seized with a very
bad attack of Crimean fever. The doctors
said that she must at once be taken to the
Sanatorium at Balaclava. Laid on a stretcher
she was carried by the soldiers up the
mountain side. For a few days it was
thought that she was dying, but presently
the joyful news was spread that she was
better. She herself says that the first thing
that helped her to recover was her joy over a

bunch of wild flowers that had been brought her. Whilst she lay ill she was visited by Lord Raglan, the Commander-in-Chief of the army, who wished to thank her for all that she had done for the troops. She would not hear of going back to England after her illness as her friends wished, but as soon as possible returned to Scutari.

In the autumn, Sevastopol fell, and this brought the war to an end. But Miss Nightingale would not return home as the hospitals were still full of sick and wounded who could not be moved. She paid another visit to the hospitals in the Crimea, and travelled from one place to another over the bad mountain roads, in a carriage which had been specially made for her. She did much for the comfort of the soldiers, who had to stay on in the Crimea, and started libraries for them and reading-huts where they could go to sit and read; lectures and classes were also provided for them, and arrangements made to enable them to send home easily money and letters to their families.

Prayer of a Patient.
Lord God, Heavenly Father!

Thou art a faithful God,
and wilt not suffer any one
to be tempted beyond what
he is able, but rather with
the temptation wilt also
make a way to escape, that
he may be able to bear it.
I supplicate Thee in my
great suffering and pain,
so shape the cross, that it
may not lay too heavily
upon me, and strengthen me
that I may bear it with
patience, and nevermore
despair of Thy mercy. O
Christ, Thou Son of the
living God! Thou hast
endured the agony of the
cross for me, and hast died
for my sins, I beseech Thee
with my whole heart, have
mercy upon me a poor
sinner, and forgive me my
transgressions, wherever I
have sinned against Thee.
Let my faith in no wise
diminish. O God Holy Ghost!
Thou true comforter in all
times of need. Keep me ever
in the spirit of patience
and supplication. Sanctify
me in my reliance upon
Thee. Turn not from me in
the hour of my death, and
lead me from this vale of

Florence Nightingale

sorrow to Thyself in
heaven. Amen.

CHAPTER TEN

Notes on Nursing: Light

LIGHT.

Light essential to both health and recovery.

It is the unqualified result of all my experience with the sick, that second only to their need of fresh air is their need of light; that, after a close room, what hurts them most is a dark room. And that it is not only light but direct sun-light they want. I had rather have the power of carrying my patient about after the sun, according to the aspect of the rooms, if circumstances permit, than let him linger in a room when the sun is off. People think the effect is upon the spirits only. This is by no means the case. The sun is not only a painter but a sculptor. You

107

admit that he does the photograph. Without going into any scientific exposition we must admit that light has quite as real and tangible effects upon the human body. But this is not all. Who has not observed the purifying effect of light, and especially of direct sunlight, upon the air of a room? Here is an observation within everybody's experience. Go into a room where the shutters are always shut, (in a sick room or a bedroom there should never be shutters shut), and though the room be uninhabited, though the air has never been polluted by the breathing of human beings, you will observe a close, musty smell of corrupt air, of air i.e. unpurified by the effect of the sun's rays. The mustiness of dark rooms and corners, indeed, is proverbial. The cheerfulness of a room, the usefulness of light in treating disease is all-important.

Aspect, view and sunlight matters of first importance to the sick.

A very high authority in hospital construction has said that people do not enough consider the difference between wards and dormitories in planning their buildings. But I go farther, and say, that healthy people never remember the difference between bed-rooms and sick-rooms, in making arrangements for the sick. To a sleeper in health it does not signify what the view is from his bed. He ought never to be in it excepting when asleep, and at night. Aspect does not very much signify either (provided the sun reach his bed-room some time in every day, to purify the air), because he ought never to be in his bed-room except during the hours when there is no sun. But the case is exactly reversed with the sick, even should they be as many hours out of their beds as you are in yours, which probably they are not. Therefore, that they should be able, without raising themselves or turning in bed, to see out of window from their beds, to see sky and sun-light at least, if you can show them nothing else, I assert to be, if not of the very first importance for recovery, at least something very near it. And you should therefore look to the position of the beds of your sick one of the very first things. If they can see out of two windows instead of one, so much the better. Again, the morning sun and the mid-day sun—the hours when they are quite certain not to be up, are of more importance to them, if a choice must be made, than the afternoon sun. Perhaps you can take them out of bed in the afternoon and set them by the window, where they can see the sun. But the best rule is, if possible, to give them direct sun-light from the moment he rises till the moment he sets.

Another great difference between the bed-room and the sick-room is, that the sleeper has a very large balance of fresh air to begin with, when he begins the night, if his room has been open all day as it ought to be; the sick man has not, because all day he has been breathing the air in the same room, and dirtying it by the emanations from himself. Far more care is therefore necessary to keep up a constant change of air in the sick room.

It is hardly necessary to add that there are acute cases, (particularly a few ophthalmic cases, and diseases where the eye is morbidly sensitive), where a subdued light is necessary. But a dark north room is inadmissible even for these. You can always moderate the light by blinds and curtains.

Heavy, thick, dark window or bed

curtains should, however, hardly ever be used for any kind of sick in this country. A light white curtain at the head of the bed is, in general, all that is necessary, and a green blind to the window, to be drawn down only when necessary.

Without sunlight, we degenerate body and mind

One of the greatest observers of human things (not physiological), says, in another language, "Where there is sun there is thought." All physiology goes to confirm this. Where is the shady side of deep valleys, there is cretinism. Where are cellars and the unsunned sides of narrow streets, there is the degeneracy and weakliness of the human race—mind and body equally degenerating. Put the pale withering plant and human being into the sun, and, if not too far gone, each will recover health and spirit.

Almost all patients lie with their faces to the light.

It is a curious thing to observe how almost all patients lie with their faces turned to the light, exactly as plants always make their faces turned to the light; a patient will even complain that it gives him pain "lying on that side." "Then why do you lie on that side?" He does not know,—but we do. It is because it is the side towards the window. A fashionable physician has recently published in a government report that he always turns his patients' faces from the light. Yes, but nature is stronger than fashionable physicians, and depend upon it she turns the faces back and towards such light as she can get. Walk through the wards of a hospital, remember the bed sides of private patients you have seen, and count how many sick you ever saw lying with their faces towards the wall.

- NOTES ON NURSING: WHAT IT IS, AND WHAT IT IS NOT by FLORENCE NIGHTINGALE. (1859)

CHAPTER ELEVEN

Lord, have mercy upon us.

Before she left the Crimea, Miss
Nightingale set up, at her own cost, a white
marble cross twenty feet high as a
monument to the dead. It was dedicated to
the memory of the soldiers who had
perished and to the nurses who had died in
tending them, and on it was written in
English and Russian, "Lord, have mercy
upon us."

From all sides she received tributes for her
services. The Sultan gave her a diamond
bracelet; Queen Victoria sent her a beautiful
jewel specially designed by Prince Albert.
Speaking in the House of Lords, Lord
Ellesmere said: "The hospitals are empty.

The angel of mercy still lingers to the last on the scene of her labours; but her mission is all but accomplished. Those long arcades of Scutari, in which dying men sat up to catch the sound of her footstep or the flutter of her dress, and fell back on the pillows content to have seen her shadow as it passed, are now comparatively deserted. She may be thinking how to escape, as best she may, on her return, the demonstration of a nation's appreciation of the deeds and motives of Florence Nightingale." This was just what Miss Nightingale wished to do. The government offered to bring her home in a man-of-war, but she travelled quietly back under the name of Miss Smith, so that her uncommon name might not attract attention to her. When she got to her own home, she went in by the back door. Crowds of people used to gather round the park in the following weeks in the hope of seeing her, but she refused to receive any sort of public welcome.

As soon as the war came to an end, before Miss Nightingale had returned home, a movement was started to give her a testimonial from the nation. Her friends had said that the only testimonial she would accept would be one which would help on the cause of providing trained nurses for the hospitals; and a Nightingale Hospital Fund was started to be given to her on her return to start her work of reform. Public meetings were held in support of this fund and when Miss Nightingale got back it had reached £48,000. With the help of friends she considered how best this money could be used. She was too ill to undertake herself as she had intended to manage the new institute for training nurses or to do more than advise from her sick room what had best be done. She had hoped that rest would completely restore her health, and even wished to go out to India to nurse when the mutiny broke out in 1857; but this was impossible. After her return from the Crimea she led almost continuously an invalid life; but it was not an idle life. She directed all the arrangements for using the Nightingale Fund, which was chiefly devoted to starting a school for training nurses at St. Thomas' Hospital in London; the Nightingale nurses will always keep alive the memory of her name. In all other matters connected with nursing she always took an active interest, especially in the health of the soldiers and in nursing in the army, and also in starting district nurses to nurse the sick poor in their own homes. Her advice was constantly sought, and she wrote many papers about nursing which were most useful, especially a very popular little book called "Notes on Nursing." But for more than fifty years since her wonderful work in the Crimea, she has lived a secluded life as an invalid, though it has been a life full of work and thought for the service of others. She is still living (in 1909) but is a complete invalid. The great lesson of her life is, that she had prepared herself so well that when the opportunity for doing a great piece of work came to her, she was able to use it. She had learnt and studied, and when the need came she was ready.

The Master's Voice.
"I will watch to see what He will say unto me."--Hab. ii. 1.

When the Lord Jesus said to Simon the Pharisee, "Simon, I have somewhat to say unto thee;" he answered,

116

"Master, say on!" When God was going to speak to Samuel, he said, "Speak, Lord, for Thy servant heareth." Has the Lord Jesus said anything like this for us? He says, "I have yet many things to say unto you." What things? They will be strong, helpful, life-giving words, for He says, "The words that I speak unto you, they are spirit and they are life." They will be very loving words, for He says, "I will speak comfortably to her" (margin, "I will speak to her heart"). And they will be very kind and tender words, and spoken just at the right moment, for He says that He knows "how to speak a word in season to him that is weary." "Will He really speak to me?" says the little heart. Yes, really, if you will only watch to see what He will say to you. For it will be "a still, small voice," and you will not hear it at all if you do not listen for it. "How will He speak to

117

me?" If I had something
very nice to tell you, and
instead of saying it out
loud, I wrote it down on a
piece of paper, and gave it
you to look at, would not
that be exactly the same as
if I had told it you with
my lips? And you would take
the paper eagerly to see
what it was that I had to
say to you. So to-day, when
you read your Bible, either
alone or at your Bible-
lesson, watch to see what
Jesus will say to you in
it. You will never really
watch in vain. You will see
some word that seems to
come home to you, and that
you never noticed so much
before. Oh, listen lovingly
to it, for that is what He
says to you! Or if you are
really watching and wishing
for a word from Him, some
sweet text will come into
your mind, and you wonder
what made you think of it!
That is the voice of Jesus
speaking to your heart.
Listen to it, and treasure
it up, and follow it; and
then watch to see what else
He will say to you. Say to

Florence Nightingale

Him, "Master, say on!"

"Master, speak! and make me
ready,
   When Thy voice is truly
heard,
With obedience glad and
steady,
   Still to follow every
word.
I am listening, Lord, for
Thee;

Florence Nightingale

CHAPTER TWELVE

Notes on Nursing: Variety

VARIETY.

Variety a means of recovery.

To any but an old nurse, or an old patient, the degree would be quite inconceivable to which the nerves of the sick suffer from seeing the same walls, the same ceiling, the same surroundings during a long confinement to one or two rooms.

The superior cheerfulness of persons suffering severe paroxysms of pain over that of persons suffering from nervous debility has often been remarked upon, and attributed to the enjoyment of the former of their intervals of respite. I incline to think that the majority of cheerful cases is to be found among those patients who are not confined to one room, whatever their suffering, and that the majority of depressed cases will be seen among those subjected to a long monotony of objects about them.

The nervous frame really suffers as much from this as the digestive organs from long monotony of diet, as e.g. the soldier from his twenty-one years' "boiled beef."

Colour and form means of recovery.
The effect in sickness of beautiful objects, of variety of objects, and especially of brilliancy of colour is hardly at all appreciated.

Such cravings are usually called the "fancies" of patients. And often doubtless patients have "fancies," as, e.g. when they desire two contradictions. But much more often, their (so called) "fancies" are the most valuable indications of what is necessary for their recovery. And it would be well if nurses would watch these (so called) "fancies" closely.

I have seen, in fevers (and felt, when I was a fever patient myself) the most acute suffering produced from the patient (in a hut) not being able to see out of window, and the knots in the wood being the only view. I shall never forget the rapture of fever patients over a bunch of bright-coloured flowers. I remember (in my own case) a nosegay of wild flowers being sent me, and from that moment recovery becoming more rapid.

This is no fancy.

People say the effect is only on the mind. It is no such thing. The effect is on the body, too. Little as we know about the way in which we are affected by form, by colour, and light, we do know this, that they have an actual physical effect.

Variety of form and brilliancy of colour in the objects presented to patients are actual means of recovery.

But it must be slow variety, e.g., if you shew a patient ten or twelve engravings successively, ten-to-one that he does not become cold and faint, or feverish, or even sick; but hang one up opposite him, one on each successive day, or week, or month, and he will revel in the variety.

Flowers.

The folly and ignorance which reign too often supreme over the sick-room, cannot be better exemplified than by this. While the nurse will leave the patient stewing in a corrupting atmosphere, the best ingredient of which is carbonic acid; she will deny him, on the plea of unhealthiness, a glass of cut-flowers, or a growing plant. Now, no one ever saw "overcrowding" by plants in a room or ward. And the carbonic acid they give off at nights would not poison a fly. Nay, in overcrowded rooms, they actually absorb carbonic acid and give off oxygen. Cut-flowers also decompose water and produce oxygen gas. It is true there are certain flowers, e.g., lilies, the smell of which is said to depress the nervous system. These are easily known by the smell, and can be avoided.

Effect of body on mind.

Volumes are now written and spoken upon the effect of the mind upon the body. Much of it is true. But I wish a little more was thought of the effect of the body on the mind. You who believe yourselves overwhelmed with anxieties, but are able every day to walk up Regent-street, or out in the country, to take your meals with others in other rooms, &c., &c., you little know how much your anxieties are thereby lightened; you little know how intensified they become to those who can have no change; how the very walls of their sick rooms seem hung with their cares; how the ghosts of their troubles haunt their beds; how impossible it is for them to escape from a pursuing thought without some help from variety.

A patient can just as much move his leg when it is fractured as change his thoughts when no external help from variety is given him. This is, indeed, one of the main sufferings of sickness; just as the fixed posture is one of the main sufferings of the broken limb.

Help the sick to vary their thoughts.
It is an ever recurring wonder to see educated people, who call themselves nurses, acting thus. They vary their own objects, their own employments many times a day; and while nursing (!) some bed-

ridden sufferer, they let him lie there staring
at a dead wall, without any change of object
to enable him to vary his thoughts; and it
never even occurs to them, at least to move
his bed so that he can look out of window.
No, the bed is to be always left in the
darkest, dullest, remotest, part of the room.

I think it is a very common error among
the well to think that "with a little more self-
control" the sick might, if they choose,
"dismiss painful thoughts" which "aggravate
their disease," &c. Believe me, almost any
sick person, who behaves decently well,
exercises more self-control every moment of
his day than you will ever know till you are
sick yourself. Almost every step that crosses
his room is painful to him; almost every
thought that crosses his brain is painful to
him; and if he can speak without being
savage, and look without being unpleasant,
he is exercising self-control.

Suppose you have been up all night, and
instead of being allowed to have your cup of
tea, you were to be told that you ought to
"exercise self-control," what should you say?
Now, the nerves of the sick are always in the

state that yours are in after you have been up all night.

Supply to the sick the defect of manual labour.

We will suppose the diet of the sick to be cared for. Then, this state of nerves is most frequently to be relieved by care in affording them a pleasant view, a judicious variety as to flowers, and pretty things. Light by itself will often relieve it. The craving for "the return of day," which the sick so constantly evince, is generally nothing but the desire for light, the remembrance of the relief which a variety of objects before the eye affords to the harassed sick mind.

Again, every man and every woman has some amount of manual employment, excepting a few fine ladies, who do not even dress themselves, and who are virtually in the same category, as to nerves, as the sick. Now, you can have no idea of the relief which manual labour is to you—of the degree to which the deprivation of manual employment increases the peculiar irritability from which many sick suffer.

A little needle-work, a little writing, a little cleaning, would be the greatest relief the sick could have, if they could do it; these are the greatest relief to you, though you do not know it. Reading, though it is often the only thing the sick can do, is not this relief. Bearing this in mind, bearing in mind that you have all these varieties of employment which the sick cannot have, bear also in mind to obtain for them all the varieties which they can enjoy.

I need hardly say that I am well aware that excess in needle-work, in writing, in any other continuous employment, will produce the same irritability that defect in manual employment (as one cause) produces in the sick.

- NOTES ON NURSING: WHAT IT IS, AND WHAT IT IS NOT by FLORENCE NIGHTINGALE. (1859)